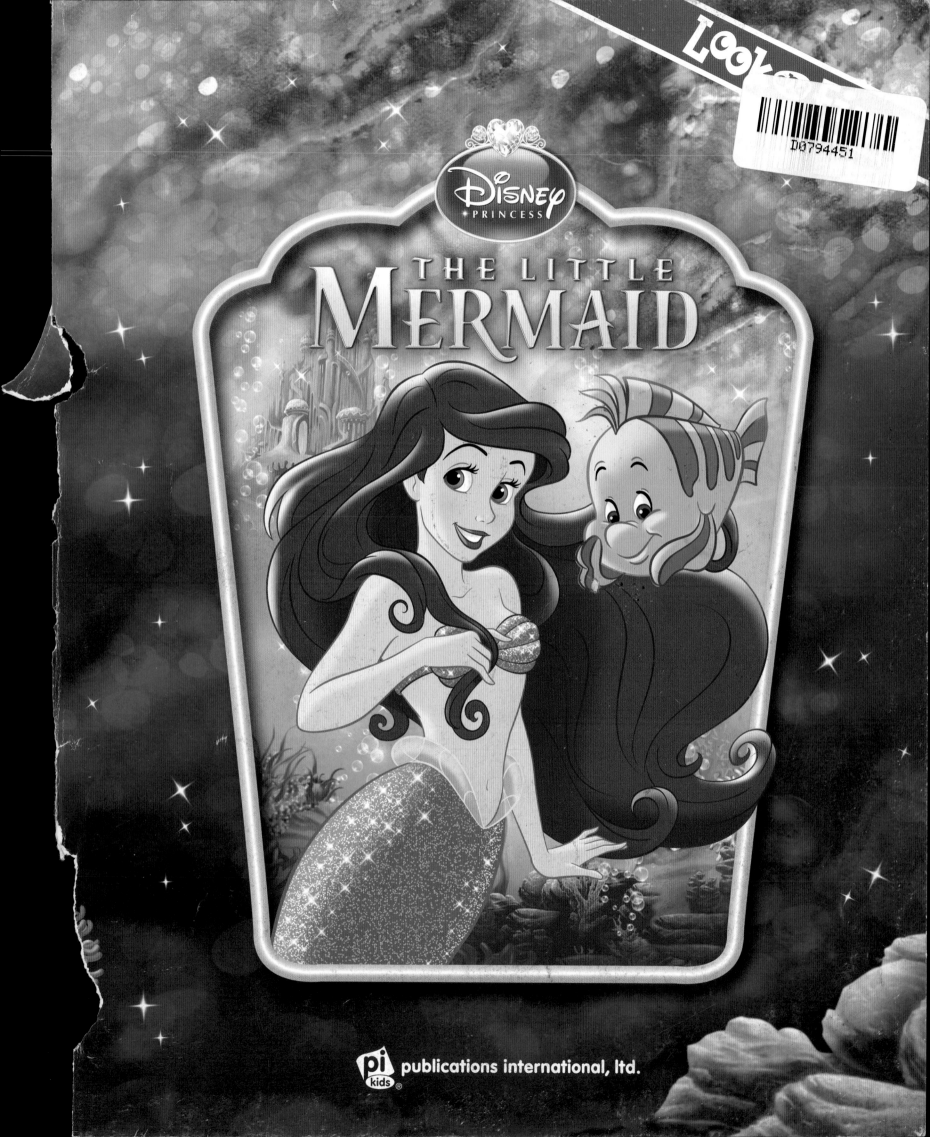

Welcome to Atlantica! King Triton bids you welcome to his kingdom under the sea. Take a look around for the king; his youngest daughter, Ariel; and these other members of his kingdom.

King Triton

Flounder

Ursula

Ariel

Sebastian

Arista

ROYAL STURGEON
GENERAL

WADING ROOM

Lightning flashes and thunder crashes as Eric's ship catches fire! Ariel remembers that people can't breathe underwater. Can you find these birthday guests and gifts while Ariel helps some humans?

Eric's Gift

A noisemaker

A party hat

A secret guest

Grimsby

Eric's cake

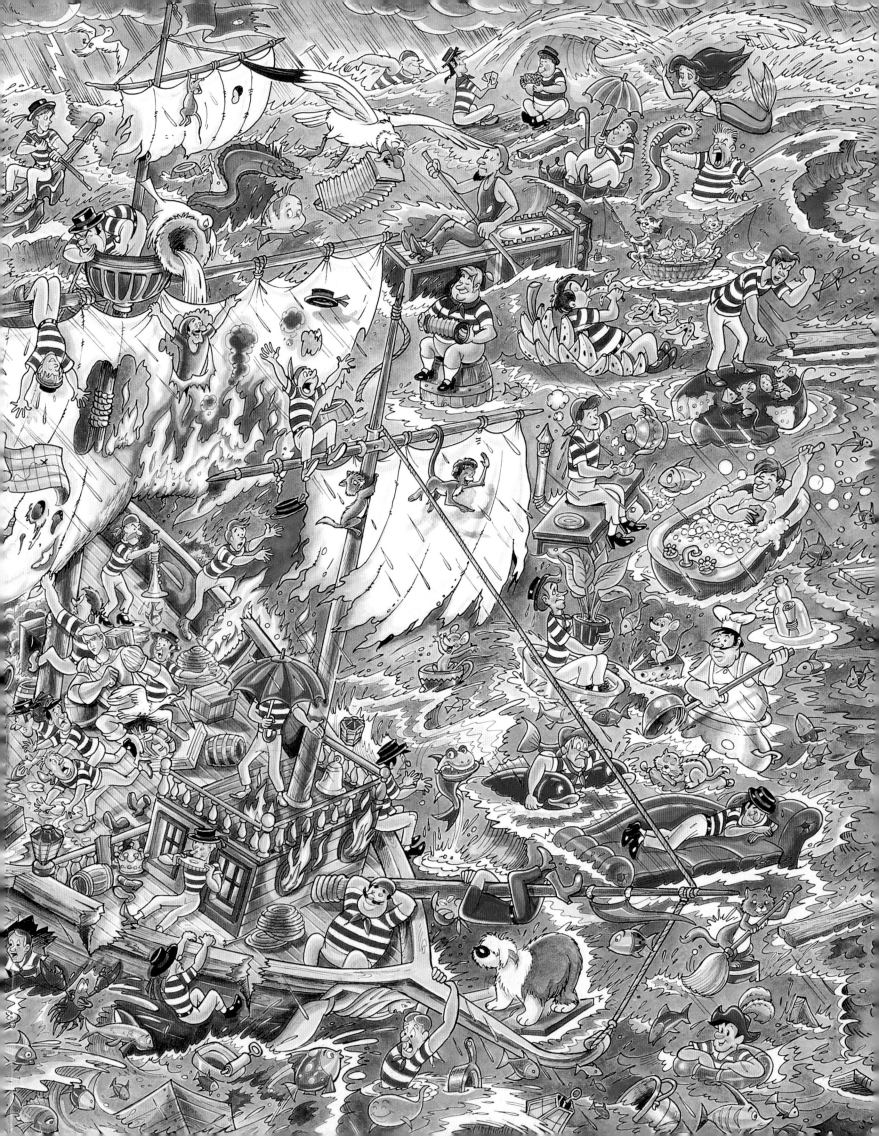

Ariel dreams of being part of the human world. But Sebastian pleads, "Ariel! Stop talking crazy! The human world is a mess. Life under the sea is better than anything they got up there!"

Can you find these fish who are trying to help convince Ariel to stay under the sea?

A parrot fish

A nurse shark

A hammerhead shark

A catfish

An oarfish

A trumpet fish

A dogfish

A clown fish

A peanut-butter-and-jellyfish

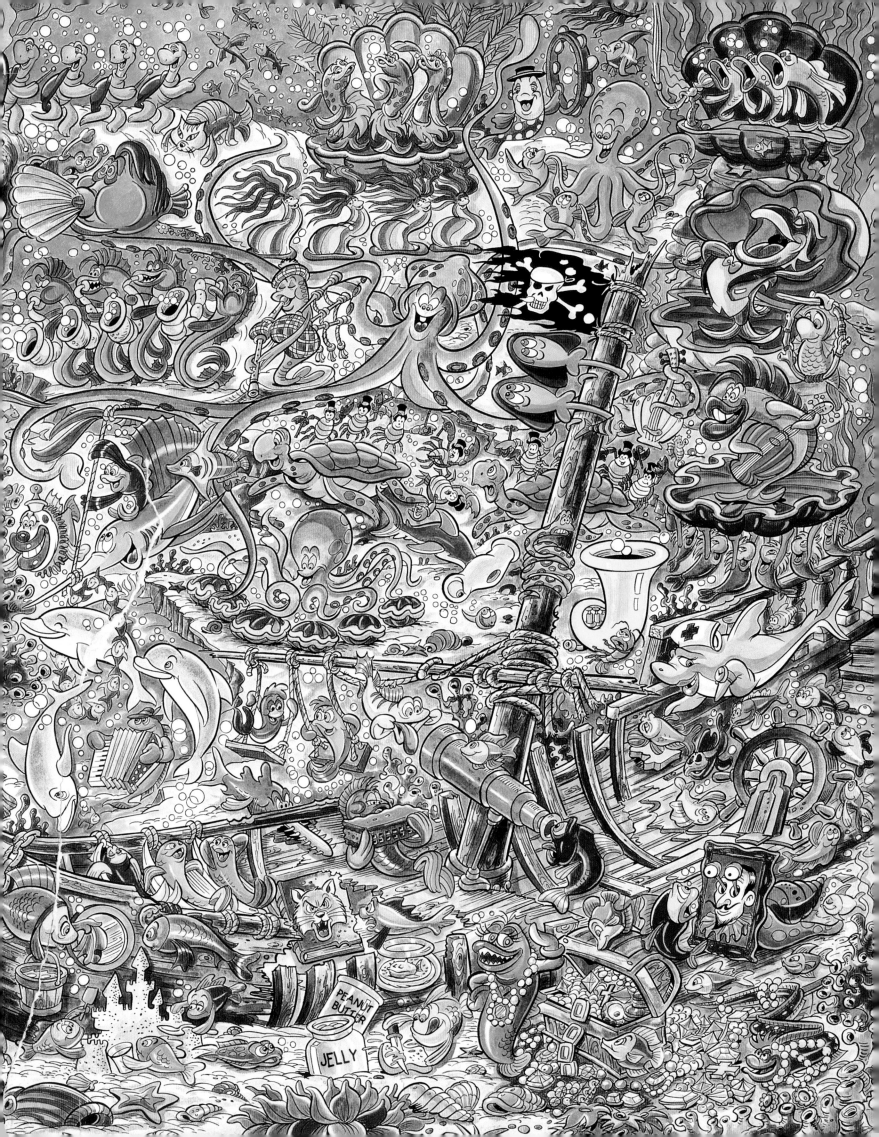

In her secret grotto, Ariel keeps a hidden treasure trove of human things. She has quite a collection! Her friend Scuttle has told her the names of many human things — but they're probably not the same names we humans use! Can you find these amazing treasures she has collected?

A snarfblatt

A squeekinsquawk

A whatzat

A tweeknose

A slurp

A dingelhopper

A snoozebuzzer

HERMIT CRAB
KEEP OUT!

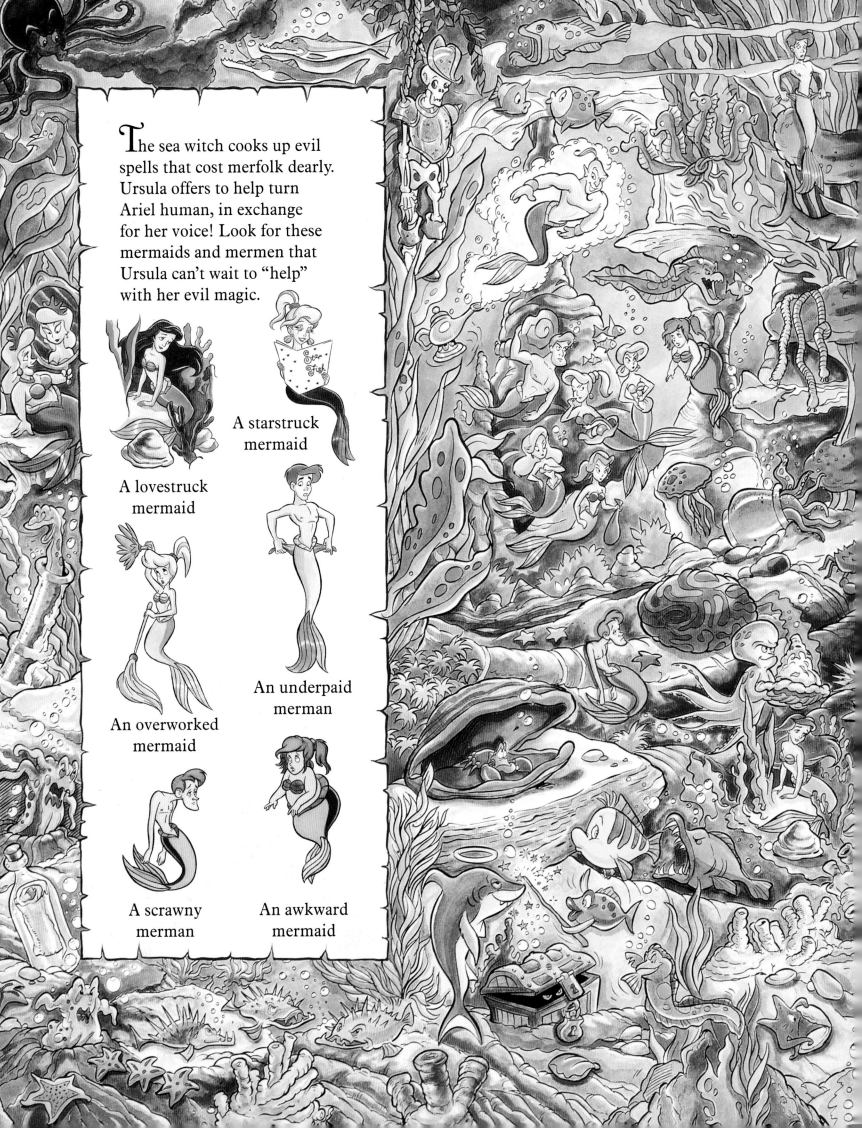

The sea witch cooks up evil spells that cost merfolk dearly. Ursula offers to help turn Ariel human, in exchange for her voice! Look for these mermaids and mermen that Ursula can't wait to "help" with her evil magic.

A lovestruck mermaid

A starstruck mermaid

An overworked mermaid

An underpaid merman

A scrawny merman

An awkward mermaid

Ariel may have made it safely to shore, but Sebastian sure hasn't! Chef Louie chases what he thinks is a runaway crab for Eric and Ariel's dinner! Find these hiding places for Sebastian as he scurries around the kitchen.

This watering can

This soup ladle

This teapot

This egg cup

This cuckoo clock

This teacup

The human world is a strange and wonderful place to Ariel. It's everything she hoped it would be, and more! Can you find these members of Eric's kingdom who are just as curious about the strange new girl as she is of them?

Chef Louie

The gatekeeper

The stable boy

Carlotta

The chambermaid

The gardener

Safe from the sea witch and in love, Eric and Ariel get married! It is a celebration like none other! Look for these wedding guests who have come from the land and the sea to wish Ariel and Eric a happy ever-after.

Chef Louie

Carlotta

Scuttle

Grimsby

Max

Sebastian

Flounder

Dive back down to King Triton's castle and look for royal subjects doing these things:

Walking a dog
Sword fighting
Hanging laundry
Clipping hedges
Teaching school
Digging for treasure

Flip back to Eric's shipwreck and look for these human things that Ariel is too busy to collect:

Teapot
Vase of flowers
Ship in a bottle
Clock
Golden crown
Treasure chest

Swim back to Sebastian's underwater orchestra. Can you find these instruments?

Kettle drum
Tuba
Tambourine
Accordion
Triangle
Harmonica
Bagpipes

Sneak back to Ariel's secret hideaway. Can you find these treasures? Can you give them silly names like Scuttle did?

Candlestick
Scissors
Bow and arrow
Baby bottle
Piggy bank
Birdcage
Horseshoe
Spinning wheel

Ursula has many kinds of magic. Can you find these magical things lying around her lair?

Crystal ball
Book of evil spells
Bottle of love potion
Magic mirror
Enchanted lamp
Magician's hat
Magic wand